P9-DGV-703

PRESIDENTS

JOHN TYLER

A MyReportLinks.com Book

Kim A. O'Connell

MyReportLinks.com Books

an imprint of

Enslow Publishers, Inc.

Box 398, 40 Industrial Road
Berkeley Heights, NJ 07922
USA

LIBRARY
FRANKLIN PIERCE COLLEGE
RINDGE, NH 03461

MyReportLinks.com Books, an imprint of Enslow Publishers, Inc.

Copyright © 2002 by Enslow Publishers, Inc.

All rights reserved.

No part of this book may be reproduced by any means
without the written permission of the publisher.

Library of Congress Cataloging-in-Publication Data

O'Connell, Kim A.
    John Tyler: A MyReportLinks.com Book / Kim A. O'Connell.
        p. cm. — (Presidents)
    Includes bibliographical references and index.
    Summary: A biography of the tenth President of the United States, under whose
administration the Treaty of Wanghia was signed, thus opening China to American
traders and paving the way for international trade that still occurs today. Includes
Internet links to Web sites, source documents, and photographs related to John Tyler.
    ISBN 0-7660-5070-X
    1. Tyler, John, 1790–1862—Juvenile literature. 2. Presidents—United
States—Biography—Juvenile literature. [1.Tyler, John, 1790–1862. 2. Presidents.]
    I. Title. II. Series.

E397 .029 2002
973.5'8'092—dc2l
[B]
                                                                2001004395

Printed in the United States of America

10 9 8 7 6 5 4 3 2 1

To Our Readers: We have done our best to make sure all Internet addresses in this book
were active and appropriate when we went to press. However, the author and the Publisher
have no control over, and assume no liability for, the material available on those Internet
sites or on other Web sites they may link to. The Publisher will try to keep the Report Links
that back up this book up to date on our Web site for three years from the book's
first publication date. Any comments or suggestions can be sent by e-mail to
comments@myreportlinks.com or to the address on the back cover.

Photo Credits: © Corel Corporation, pp. 1 (background), 3; Courtesy of American
Memory, the Library of Congress, p. 13; Courtesy of Bartleby.com, p. 43; Courtesy of
DiscoverySchool.com, p. 20; Courtesy of Encyclopedia Americana, p. 11; Courtesy
of HistoryCentral.com, p. 18; Courtesy of Sherwood Forest Plantation, pp. 39, 41;
Courtesy of The American Presidency, p. 26; Courtesy of The American President, p. 30;
Courtesy of the Tyler family, p. 4; Courtesy of The White House, pp. 32, 35; The Adam
Smith Institute, p. 16; The Library of Congress, pp. 17, 20, 25, 28, 33, 37.

Cover Photo: © Corel Corporation; Courtesy of the Tyler family.

Contents

MyReportLinks.com Books
Great Books, Great Links, Great for Research!

MyReportLinks.com Books present the information you need to learn about your report subject. In addition, they show you where to go on the Internet for more information. The pre-evaluated Report Links, listed on **www.myreportlinks.com**, save hours of research time and link to dozens—even hundreds—of Web sites, source documents, and photos related to your report topic.

To Our Readers:
Each Report Link has been reviewed by our editors, who will work hard to keep only active and appropriate Internet addresses in our books and up to date on our Web site. However, the author and the Publisher have no control over, and assume no liability for, the material available on those Internet sites, or on other Web sites they may link to.

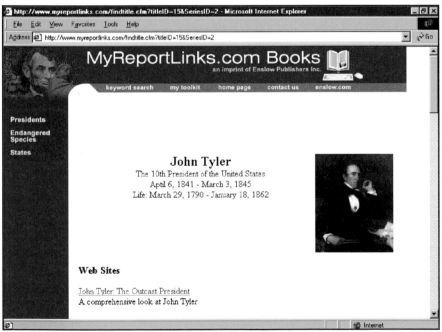

Access:
The Publisher will try to keep the Report Links that back up this book up to date on our Web site for three years from the book's first publication date. Please enter **PTY1262** if asked for a password.

> The Internet sites described below can be accessed at
> **http://www.myreportlinks.com**

▶**John Tyler: The Outcast President**   *EDITOR'S CHOICE

This site provides a comprehensive look at John Tyler before, during,
and after his presidency.

Link to this Internet site from http://www.myreportlinks.com
*EDITOR'S CHOICE

▶**The Internet Public Library: John Tyler**

This site contains interesting facts, such as the names of Tyler's fifteen
children, all of the government positions he held, and lists the names of
the members of his cabinet.

Link to this Internet site from http://www.myreportlinks.com
*EDITOR'S CHOICE

▶**The American Presidency: John Tyler**

This site details Tyler's early rise in politics, his nomination for the
vice-presidency, and the domestic and foreign policies he created
as president.

Link to this Internet site from http://www.myreportlinks.com
*EDITOR'S CHOICE

▶**Heir to an Insurrection**

This site describes Tyler's firsts: He was the first vice president to
succeed a fallen president, the first president to become married in
office, and the first president to face impeachment.

Link to this Internet site from http://www.myreportlinks.com
*EDITOR'S CHOICE

▶**Sherwood Forest**

Tyler lived here with his wife from 1842 until his death in 1862. You
will find photos and details of the history of the house and can take a
"virtual tour."

Link to this Internet site from http://www.myreportlinks.com
*EDITOR'S CHOICE

▶**The American Presidency**

At this site you will find objects related to all the presidents of the
United States. You can also read a brief description of the era Tyler lived
in and learn about the office of the presidency.

Link to this Internet site from http://www.myreportlinks.com

Report Links

 The Internet sites described below can be accessed at
http://www.myreportlinks.com

The American Presidency: Whig Party
This site describes the history of the Whig Party, including the party's support for John Tyler and its eventual removal of him from the ranks.

Link to this Internet site from http://www.myreportlinks.com

A Brief History of Texas
The history of Texas is given, including the 1844 treaty that called for the annexation of the state.

Link to this Internet site from http://www.myreportlinks.com

Election of 1840
The election of 1840 is explained, including a breakdown of nominees, electoral college votes, and popular votes.

Link to this Internet site from http://www.myreportlinks.com

"I Do Solemnly Swear . . ."
This site contains an image of John Tyler, then vice president, receiving the news of President William Henry Harrison's death.

Link to this Internet site from http://www.myreportlinks.com

Impeachment: The Process and History
This site explains the impeachment process and profiles the four United States presidents who have faced impeachment.

Link to this Internet site from http://www.myreportlinks.com

John Tyler
Encyclopedia Britannica Intermediate provides a brief introduction to the life of John Tyler.

Link to this Internet site from http://www.myreportlinks.com

Any comments? Contact us: **comments@myreportlinks.com**

Report Links

 The Internet sites described below can be accessed at
http://www.myreportlinks.com

▶**John Tyler: 10th President of the United States**
Tyler's belief in states' rights and limited power for the federal
government are described. A letter from Tyler resigning his seat in the
Senate is included.

Link to this Internet site from http://www.myreportlinks.com

▶**John Tyler: (1841–1845) Whig**
Tyler's early life, his career path, the domestic and foreign relations
problems in his administration, and his later years are described.

Link to this Internet site from http://www.myreportlinks.com

▶**John Tyler and the Pursuit of National Destiny**
This essay, reprinted from the *Journal of the Early American Republic*,
explores John Tyler's views on national destiny.

Link to this Internet site from http://www.myreportlinks.com

▶**Letitia Tyler**
Although ill for much of her married life, Tyler's first wife, Letitia, was
nonetheless regarded as an affectionate mother. This site describes her
early life and contains quotations about her from her daughter-in-law.

Link to this Internet site from http://www.myreportlinks.com

▶**Life Portraits: John Tyler**
Personal and public "Life Facts" and "Did you know?" trivia on Tyler
are listed, including a link to a letter Tyler wrote to his thirteen-year-old
daughter Mary.

Link to this Internet site from http://www.myreportlinks.com

▶**Monroe Doctrine**
In 1842, Tyler extended the Monroe Doctrine to include the Hawaiian
Islands, in order to lessen British interest there.

Link to this Internet site from http://www.myreportlinks.com

Report Links

The Internet sites described below can be accessed at
http://www.myreportlinks.com

Mr. President
By navigating through this site you will find brief descriptions of all United States presidents.

Link to this Internet site from http://www.myreportlinks.com

The National Portrait Gallery: John Tyler
An oil-on-canvas portrait of Tyler painted by George P. A. Healy in 1859 is featured.

Link to this Internet site from http://www.myreportlinks.com

Presidential Children: Tyler's 15, Still A Record
This article discusses the many children John Tyler had with wives Letitia and Julia. Here you will learn about the lives of Tyler's children.

Link to this Internet site from http://www.myreportlinks.com

Presidents Who Were Not Inaugurated
John Tyler was one of five presidents who were not inaugurated. Here you can read about those presidents.

Link to this Internet site from http://www.myreportlinks.com

Sherwood Forest Personality: President John Tyler
A brief overview of John Tyler's life—including his family, his political career, his term as president, and his legacy—is given in this site.

Link to this Internet site from http://www.myreportlinks.com

Tyler, John
At this site you will find basic information about John Tyler's early career, his presidency, and his later years.

Link to this Internet site from http://www.myreportlinks.com

Report Links

The Internet sites described below can be accessed at
http://www.myreportlinks.com

▶ Tyler, John (1790–1862)
Listed are the important events in Tyler's life with details of his political
career, administration, and later years.

Link to this Internet site from http://www.myreportlinks.com

▶ Tyler, Julia Gardiner (1820–1889)
Julia Gardiner married John Tyler in 1844, making it the first time a
president married while in office. This site describes her family life and
her role as the first lady, including her custom of having musicians play
"Hail to the Chief" when the president appeared at public events.

Link to this Internet site from http://www.myreportlinks.com

▶ Vice Presidents of the United States: John Tyler (1841)
This site emphasizes Tyler's role in the 1840 election and his short term
as vice president. It also includes excerpts from his vice presidential
inaugural address.

Link to this Internet site from http://www.myreportlinks.com

▶ Visiting John Tyler's Grave
In addition to showing Tyler's gravesite, this site provides an overview
of Tyler, highlighting some aspects of his life and presidency.

Link to this Internet site from http://www.myreportlinks.com

▶ The White House Historical Association
By navigating through this site you will find information on John Tyler
and other United States presidents. You can also take a virtual tour of
the White House.

Link to this Internet site from http://www.myreportlinks.com

▶ The White House: John Tyler
This useful and concise biography of Tyler contains "Fun Facts" and
"Fast Facts."

Link to this Internet site from http://www.myreportlinks.com

Highlights

1790—*March 29:* Born in Charles City County, Virginia.

1802—Enrolls in William and Mary College.

1807—Graduates from William and Mary College.

1809—Admitted to the bar to practice law.

1811–1816—Serves as member of Virginia legislature.

1813—*March 29:* Marries Letitia Christian.

1813—Named captain of militia company in War of 1812.

1816–1821—Serves as U.S. representative from Virginia.

1825–1827—Serves as governor of Virginia.

1827–1836—Serves as U.S. senator from Virginia.

1836—Runs for vice president and loses.

1838–1840—Returns to serve in Virginia legislature.

1840—Running on the "Tippecanoe and Tyler Too" ticket, elected vice president.

1841—*April 6:* Sworn in as the tenth U.S. president, after William Henry Harrison dies in office.

1842—*Sept. 10:* Letitia dies after a long illness.

1842—Webster-Ashburton Treaty settles boundary disputes and opens way for westward expansion.

1842—Treaty of Wanghia is signed, opening trade with China.

1844—Warship *Princeton* explodes, killing two cabinet members and Tyler's would-be father-in-law.

—*June 26:* Marries Julia Gardiner.

1845—Signs congressional resolution annexing Texas.

1861—Named chair of peace conference in Washington, D.C.

1862—After Virginia secedes, named member of Confederate Congress.

—*Jan. 18:* Dies, in Richmond, Virginia.

Chapter 1 ▶

The Accidental President

The presidential inauguration of 1841 fell on a very cold and raw March day. But the weather did not stop newly elected president William Henry Harrison from riding his favorite horse to the Capitol building in Washington, D.C., to be sworn in. He wore no coat and held his hat in

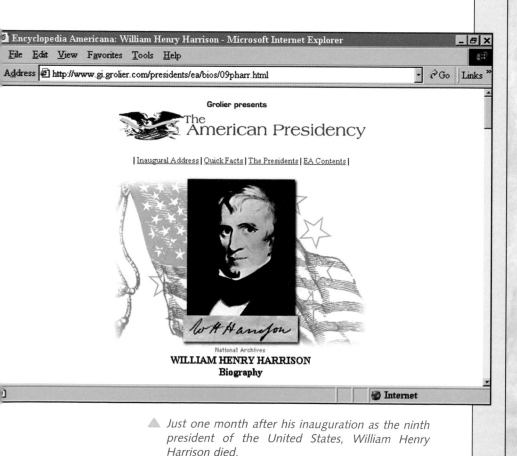

Encyclopedia Americana: William Henry Harrison - Microsoft Internet Explorer

File   Edit   View   Favorites   Tools   Help

Address http://www.gi.grolier.com/presidents/ea/bios/09pharr.html   Go   Links

Grolier presents

The American Presidency

| Inaugural Address | Quick Facts | The Presidents | EA Contents |

National Archives

WILLIAM HENRY HARRISON
Biography

Internet

▲ Just one month after his inauguration as the ninth president of the United States, William Henry Harrison died.

his hand. At sixty-eight, he was the oldest president ever elected, and he wanted to appear strong. Everywhere he turned, he shook hands and greeted onlookers in the huge crowd. Once he arrived at the Capitol, Harrison stood in the wintry weather for more than an hour and a half, delivering his inaugural speech.

Not surprisingly, Harrison became ill. What had begun as a cold, however, soon developed into pneumonia. After a week of feeling gravely ill, Harrison seemed to recover somewhat, but then his condition worsened. On April 4, 1841, only a month after he had been inaugurated, William Henry Harrison died.

This shocking turn of events threw the new administration into turmoil. No president had ever died in office. No one was sure what to do. Members of Harrison's cabinet assumed that the new vice president would take over. They immediately wrote a letter to John Tyler. At the time, however, Tyler was at his home in Williamsburg, Virginia, unaware of the situation.

Tyler had little contact with Harrison during the campaign. He was prepared to be a behind-the-scenes vice president, allowing the president to do his job without much assistance from him. Tyler's political party, the Whigs, did not mind this attitude. When Tyler decided to stay in Virginia a little longer, even after the election, it was not considered a problem.

So Tyler was surprised to hear someone banging on the front door of his home at sunrise on April 5. A flustered Fletcher Webster, son of Secretary of State Daniel Webster, was there. He had ridden all night to bring dispatches from Washington. "My God, the president is dead!" Tyler exclaimed when he glanced at the papers. "Yes, sir, Mr. President," Webster replied, "the nation is in mourning."[1]

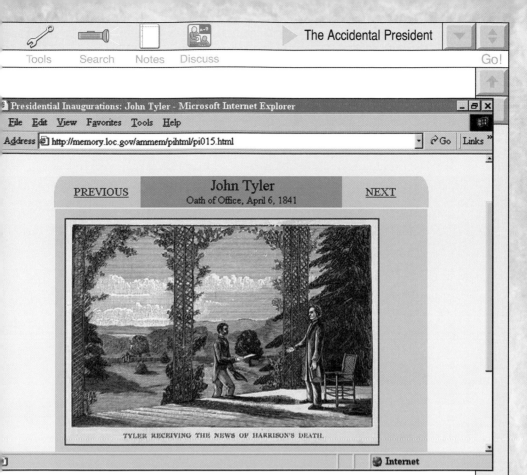

PREVIOUS   **John Tyler**   NEXT
Oath of Office, April 6, 1841

TYLER RECEIVING THE NEWS OF HARRISON'S DEATH.

Internet

At sunrise, on April 5, 1841, a messenger who had ridden all night delivered a stunning message to John Tyler: President Harrison was dead and he, John Tyler, was soon to be sworn in as the president of the United States.

In only a moment, Tyler had gone from being asleep to being addressed as "Mr. President." As vice president, he may have been prepared to accept his new role, but could he have been ready for what awaited him in the nation's capital? He did not have much time to think about it. Less than a day later, he was in a Washington hotel, being sworn in as the tenth president of the United States.

Chapter 2 ▶

Tyler's Early Life, 1790–1809

At the end of the 1700s, tobacco farming was a booming business in Virginia. In the lowlands along the Chesapeake Bay, known as Tidewater Virginia, tobacco fields were everywhere. The families that owned those fields were the richest and most respected in the region. The Tylers were one of those families.

▶ Southern Beginnings

The Tylers lived on a large 1,200-acre estate along the James River that they called Greenway. The patriarch of the family was John Tyler, Sr., who became famous during the Revolutionary War. He was an outspoken member of the Virginia legislature, where he fought for laws that protected individual rights. He was also a strong supporter of the Bill of Rights to the U.S. Constitution. Later, John Tyler, Sr., was also a governor of Virginia, from 1809 to 1811, and a federal judge. Throughout his career, Judge Tyler, as he was most often called, emphasized the importance of personal rights. But like many other Southerners at that time, Judge Tyler did not extend this belief to slaves. He owned slaves his entire life.

Into this world of tobacco, politics, and slavery, a future president was born. On March 29, 1790, John and Mary Armistead Tyler welcomed their son John into the world. He was one of eight children. Young John was a small boy with a thin face, long nose, and high cheekbones. Always too small and too thin, Tyler fell ill regularly. He had a serious childhood marked by the great loss of his mother, who died of a stroke when John was only seven.

But there were happy times too. Judge Tyler took his young son under his wing, teaching him a love of music and storytelling. John Tyler liked to sit on the front lawn of Greenway, in the shadow of a large willow tree, while his father played the violin or told heroic tales of the Revolutionary War. John soon learned to play the fiddle himself. He also began to listen closely to his father's concerns about personal rights.

Education

Despite his small build, John held his own at school. According to one legend, he stood up to a cruel school-master, Mr. McMurdo, who whipped his students if they fell out of line. As the story goes, John led other boys in a revolt in which they physically overpowered McMurdo. Although John Tyler would later not admit that such a revolt had happened, he did say that he was surprised that McMurdo "did not whip all the sense out of his scholars."[1]

In 1802, at the age of twelve, John left home to enroll in the secondary division of the College of William and Mary in Williamsburg, Virginia. In less than four short years, he began college-level studies. He studied subjects that awakened his interest in the world around him— history, government, economics, and literature. One book in particular influenced him. In *The Wealth of Nations*, by Adam Smith, John Tyler read that the government should not get involved in a private person's business. Those words echoed what his father had been saying all along.

John's report cards from college were very promising. Although Judge Tyler was happy with his son's school

The Author of the Wealth of Nations

▲ *The Scotsman Adam Smith is generally regarded as being the father ot modern economics. John Tyler was particularly influenced by the economic ideas Smith proposed in his book* The Wealth of Nations, *published in 1776. Smith believed that the most productive economies were the result of individual freedoms.*

Edmund Randolph was the nation's first attorney general, serving in George Washington's administration. In 1809, John Tyler moved to Richmond to work in Randolph's law office. The two men held very different political views. Randolph supported a strong central government while Tyler was a proponent of states' rights.

record, he did scold him about his poor handwriting. "I can't help telling you how much I am mortified to find no improvement in your handwriting," the judge wrote to his son, "neither do you connect your lines straight, which makes your letters look so abominable."[2]

In 1807, John graduated at the young age of 17. Now bent on a political career, John Tyler returned home to study law, first under his father's guidance and then with his cousin, Chancellor Samuel Tyler. In 1809, Tyler moved to Richmond to work in the law office of Edmund Randolph. The nation's first attorney general under President George Washington, Randolph had completely different beliefs than Tyler's father had. Randolph believed in a strong central government. Tyler disagreed with Randolph's views. In fact, they served to strengthen the importance Tyler already placed on the rights of states and of individuals. Armed with an education in law and a strong belief system, Tyler was ready to enter politics.

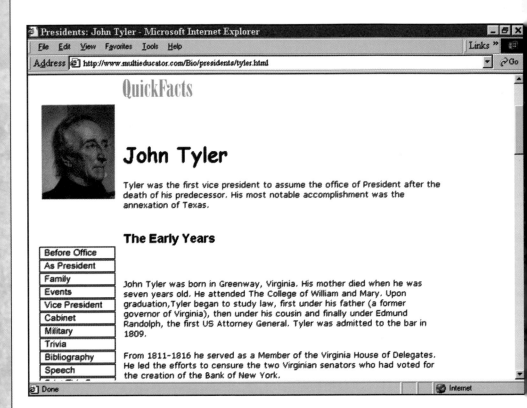

Presidents: John Tyler - Microsoft Internet Explorer

File   Edit   View   Favorites   Tools   Help   Links »

Address http://www.multieducator.com/Bio/presidents/tyler.html   ⌀Go

QuickFacts

John Tyler

Tyler was the first vice president to assume the office of President after the death of his predecessor. His most notable accomplishment was the annexation of Texas.

The Early Years

Before Office
As President
Family
Events
Vice President
Cabinet
Military
Trivia
Bibliography
Speech

John Tyler was born in Greenway, Virginia. His mother died when he was seven years old. He attended The College of William and Mary. Upon graduation, Tyler began to study law, first under his father (a former governor of Virginia), then under his cousin and finally under Edmund Randolph, the first US Attorney General. Tyler was admitted to the bar in 1809.

From 1811-1816 he served as a Member of the Virginia House of Delegates. He led the efforts to censure the two Virginian senators who had voted for the creation of the Bank of New York.

Done   Internet

▲ *In 1809, John Tyler was admitted to the Virginia bar, that state's association of lawyers.*

Chapter 3 ▶

Journey to the White House, 1811–1841

As Judge Tyler was ending his term as governor of Virginia, his son was about to enter Virginia politics. In 1811, John Tyler was elected to the Virginia House of Delegates as the representative of Charles City County. He was not there long before he began to make his mark.

▶ Political Beginnings

The legislature was discussing whether the United States should continue to have a national bank. The First Bank of the United States had been founded in 1791. It was originally chartered to help the new nation pay off its war debt after the American Revolution. Its supporters thought that a national bank would be a safe way to handle the government's money. But its detractors, including John Tyler, thought the bank's branches in the states gave the government another way to control the states and limit their power. The Virginia legislature ordered the state's two U.S. senators to vote against the bank, but they would not. Outraged, Tyler wanted them to be punished. He introduced a bill stating that a state legislature could tell that state's U.S. senators how to vote, and the bill passed. In 1811, Congress voted to abandon the bank's charter.

▶ Marriage

Now that Tyler had successfully begun his political career, he felt ready to marry his longtime girlfriend, Letitia Christian. Like Tyler, Letitia came from a wealthy

plantation family in Virginia—but her family's fortune was so great that it made the Tylers' fortune seem modest. Despite her wealth, however, Letitia was not proud or showy. She preferred to stay home, engaged in activities such as reading, knitting, and sewing. Friends often said that she was sweet and unselfish.

In the days before Christmas 1812, Tyler expressed his feelings for Letitia in a letter to her. He told her how happy he was that she loved him, even though he was not as rich as she was. "To ensure to you happiness is now my only

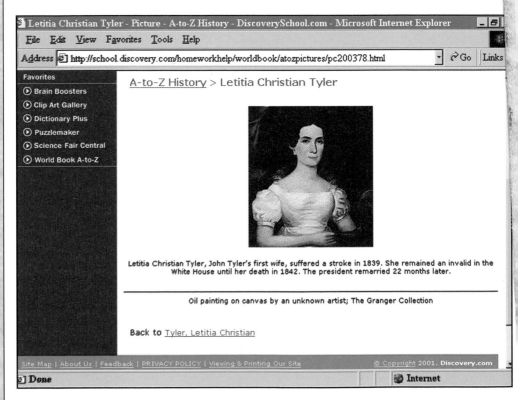

Letitia Christian Tyler - Picture - A-to-Z History - DiscoverySchool.com - Microsoft Internet Explorer

File   Edit   View   Favorites   Tools   Help

Address http://school.discovery.com/homeworkhelp/worldbook/atozpictures/pc200378.html   Go   Links

Favorites
- Brain Boosters
- Clip Art Gallery
- Dictionary Plus
- Puzzlemaker
- Science Fair Central
- World Book A-to-Z

A-to-Z History > Letitia Christian Tyler

Letitia Christian Tyler, John Tyler's first wife, suffered a stroke in 1839. She remained an invalid in the White House until her death in 1842. The president remarried 22 months later.

Oil painting on canvas by an unknown artist; The Granger Collection

Back to Tyler, Letitia Christian

Site Map | About Us | Feedback | PRIVACY POLICY | Viewing & Printing Our Site   © Copyright 2001, Discovery.com

Done   Internet

Letitia Christian married John Tyler on March 29, 1813. Like Tyler, Letitia came from a wealthy Virginia family.

object," Tyler wrote, "and whether I float or sink in the stream of fortune, you may be assured of this, that I shall never cease to love you."[1]

Three months later, on March 29, 1813, John Tyler married Letitia Christian. He told a friend before the wedding that he had expected to be nervous but he wasn't. At twenty-three years of age, Tyler had already been through college and law school and had entered politics. So for him, an important decision like marriage was not as scary as it might have been for other men his age. Tyler and Letitia moved into part of the Greenway estate to begin their married life.

"Captain Tyler"

Instead of a life of peace, however, Tyler was soon faced with war. When the War of 1812 erupted, Tyler rallied with other Americans to fight the British. He joined a company that was part of the Fifty-second Regiment of the Virginia Militia. As captain, the headstrong Tyler created a military training system that the militia members, who were mostly local farmers, could understand. The closest the unit ever came to seeing combat occurred one evening when they were stationed in Williamsburg. A rumor had circulated that British troops were entering the town. To escape the building in which they were sleeping, Tyler and his fellow soldiers rushed out of an upstairs room so quickly that they all tumbled down a staircase, landing in a heap on the floor. The British troops never appeared, and Tyler's regiment never saw action. But he was always the first to laugh if someone teased him by calling him "Captain Tyler."[2]

▶ Congressman Tyler

In 1815, the Tylers' first child, a daughter, was born. As Tyler's family began to grow, so did his political goals. The following year, he was elected to the House of Representatives and moved to Washington, D.C. As a well-known young politician and the son of a prominent Virginia family, Tyler made many important friends—including President James Madison and First Lady Dolley Madison. After eating a fancy French meal with them one evening, he wrote home to Letitia that he would "much rather dine at home in our plain way . . . with their sauces and flum-flummeries, the victuals are intolerable."[3]

As a congressman, Tyler vowed to listen to the "voice of a majority of the people."[4] But he promised to ignore the voice of the majority if he felt it violated the U.S. Constitution. His first major test in the House of Representatives again focused on the national bank. (With the closing of the First Bank of the United States, in 1811, there had ceased to be a national bank until 1816, when the Second Bank of the United States received its charter.) With grain prices dropping and the young country on the verge of a financial depression, many thought that the bank was not handling the government's money well. Tyler became a member of a congressional committee to study the bank. In a speech before the House, Tyler said that government money should be managed in state banks. Although Congress rejected this idea, Tyler's stance on states' rights was stronger than ever.

Tyler's next challenge focused on a practice that he had known his whole life—slavery. At the time, the young nation was continuing to grow, with new states being added to the Union on a regular basis. But Congress was debating whether the government had the right to say whether slavery could continue in new states. In the Missouri Compromise of 1820, Congress proposed that the new state of Maine be admitted as a free state, while the new state of Missouri would be admitted as a slave state. This way, the number of free states and slave states would remain the same, with free states in the North and slave states in the South. But Tyler considered this compromise to be further evidence that the federal government wanted to tell the South how to live. When the Missouri Compromise passed by a vote of 134 to 42, Tyler was one of the 42 who voted against it.

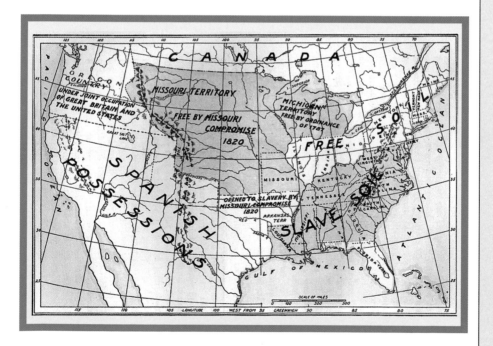

▲ This map of the United States in 1820 shows how free and slave states and territories lined up after the Missouri Compromise.

From the Capitol to the Governor's Mansion

In January 1821, Tyler resigned from Congress for health reasons. He had suffered from several illnesses in the previous year, which the stresses of politics surely did not help. He returned to his home in Charles City to practice law, eager to live a quiet life once more. But that was soon about to change again.

In 1825, Tyler followed in his father's footsteps by becoming governor of Virginia. As governor, Tyler encouraged the state to create a system of public schools for the children of Virginia. He also recommended a system of canals and roads to connect cities throughout the state. As he had in Washington, Tyler had many friends in Richmond, the state capital. When he resigned as governor, in January 1827, he was in debt because he and Letitia had held so many parties in the governor's mansion.

Choosing Sides

But financial problems soon faded from Tyler's mind when duty called him back to Washington. In early 1827, Tyler reported for work as a U.S. senator. His first task was to choose which presidential candidate he would support. His main choices were Andrew Jackson, a famous politician and general, and the current president, John Quincy Adams. Tyler did not like either candidate very well, but he thought Jackson was the better choice. Tyler disagreed with several of Jackson's views, however. For example, the general supported using federal government money to improve roads and canals—a power that Tyler thought belonged to the states.

The presidential campaign of 1828 turned out to be one of the dirtiest in history. Adams's supporters called

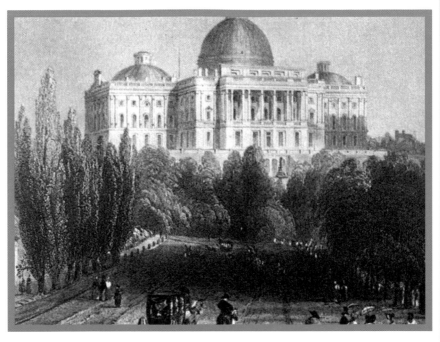

▲ *In 1827, John Tyler reported for work as a United States senator from Virginia. This painting, done that year, shows how the Capitol looked when Tyler was a member of the Senate.*

Jackson a drunken fighter, while Jackson's supporters said Adams had used government money for his own use. When it was all over, Jackson had won. "When the general comes [to Washington], we may expect more bustle and stir,"[5] Tyler wrote to a friend. And a stir is exactly what Tyler got.

In 1832, President Jackson signed into law a moderate protective tariff that angered South Carolina and other southern states. Protective tariffs were taxes on imported goods. People in the agricultural South favored low tariffs, while people in the more industrial North favored high tariffs. In response to the tariffs, the state of South Carolina voted for nullification—the practice of setting

aside a law that had already been passed by Congress. Although Tyler, a Southerner, supported states' rights and was against protective tariffs, he was also against nullification. In response to South Carolina's actions, Jackson supported a bill that would allow the use of military force against nullifiers. Yet out of thirty-three senators, Tyler was the only senator who voted against Jackson's bill, favoring instead a gradual reduction in tariffs. Many other senators did not support the bill, but they withdrew from the vote, not wanting the president to know they had

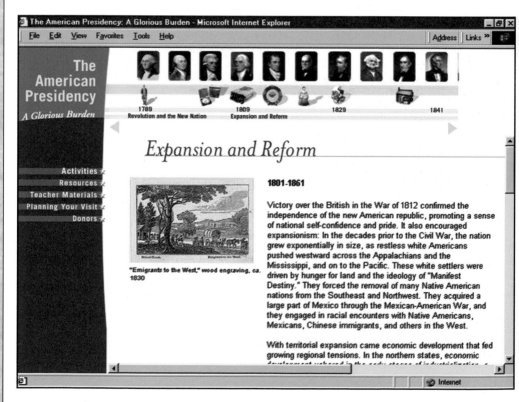

The American Presidency: A Glorious Burden - Microsoft Internet Explorer

File Edit View Favorites Tools Help   Address | Links »

The
American
Presidency
A Glorious Burden

1789
Revolution and the New Nation

1809
Expansion and Reform

1829

1841

Activities
Resources
Teacher Materials
Planning Your Visit
Donors

Expansion and Reform

"Emigrants to the West," wood engraving, ca. 1830

1801-1861

Victory over the British in the War of 1812 confirmed the independence of the new American republic, promoting a sense of national self-confidence and pride. It also encouraged expansionism: In the decades prior to the Civil War, the nation grew exponentially in size, as restless white Americans pushed westward across the Appalachians and the Mississippi, and on to the Pacific. These white settlers were driven by hunger for land and the ideology of "Manifest Destiny." They forced the removal of many Native American nations from the Southeast and Northwest. They acquired a large part of Mexico through the Mexican-American War, and they engaged in racial encounters with Native Americans, Mexicans, Chinese immigrants, and others in the West.

With territorial expansion came economic development that fed growing regional tensions. In the northern states, economic

In the first part of the nineteenth century, the United States was beginning to grow. New states were being added to the Union, and westward expansion was continuing. In this time period, John Tyler married, served briefly in the War of 1812, and was elected a congressman, a governor, and a senator.

sided against him. Tyler alone had enough courage to let his vote be known.

Tyler's concerns about Jackson soon came to a head. Once again, the issue involved the national bank. Like Tyler, Jackson opposed the bank. So in 1836, Jackson removed the existing funds and placed them in state banks. Although Tyler thought the national bank did not give states enough power, he also did not believe the president had the right to make all the decisions about government funds. Tyler voted to censure—or officially disapprove of—Jackson's actions. But the Virginia law that Tyler had supported earlier came back to haunt him. That law, which allowed the legislature to tell its U.S. representatives how to vote, now called for him to take back his censure of Jackson. Rather than disobey the legislature, Tyler resigned from the Senate. He was soon back at his new home in Williamsburg, practicing law and tending to his large family, which had grown to eight children.

▶ "Tippecanoe and Tyler Too"

But people back in Washington had not forgotten Tyler. The Whigs, an anti-Jackson political party, counted John Tyler as one of their own. In 1836, the Whigs nominated him as one of several candidates for vice president. But he did no campaigning and gave no speeches. When the votes were tallied, Tyler lost. He carried only four southern states, failing to win even his home state of Virginia.

Four years later, however, Tyler threw his hat into the ring again. This time, the Whigs nominated William Henry Harrison for president, with Tyler as the vice presidential nominee. Nicknamed "Old Tippecanoe," Harrison was hailed as the hero of an 1811 battle with a group of American Indians along the Tippecanoe River in

▲ William Henry Harrison was nicknamed "Old Tippecanoe" after winning the Battle of Tippecanoe, in 1811. At the time, Harrison was the governor of the Indiana Territory. In the 1840 presidential campaign, Harrison was portrayed as the frontier candidate—even though he had been raised on a large estate in Virginia and his home in Ohio was a twenty-two–room mansion. With Tyler added to the ticket, the slogan "Tippecanoe and Tyler Too" became a catchphrase of the campaign.

Indiana. Harrison and Tyler ran on the famous ticket known as "Tippecanoe and Tyler Too." The wild campaign even included a catchy song: "What has caused this great commotion, motion, our country through? It is the ball a-rolling on, for Tippecanoe and Tyler too, Tippecanoe and Tyler too."[6]

Harrison and Tyler won easily. When Tyler was sworn in as vice president, he urged the Senate to maintain a balance between the powers of the government and the rights of states and the people. Then he returned home, not expecting that in one month he would be handed the most important job of his life.

A Bed of Thorns: The Presidency, 1841–1845

Upon William Henry Harrison's sudden death, Tyler was thrust into the presidency with no warning. He never even gave an inaugural speech. Although many thought the Constitution clearly stated that the vice president should take over in the event of the president's death, some people in Washington insisted on calling Tyler an "acting

The American President: "Happenstance" - Microsoft Internet Explorer

File Edit View Favorites Tools Help   Links »

Address http://www.pbs.org/wnet/amerpres/main_episode02.html   Go

PBS Home   Search   Programs A-Z   TV Schedules   Shop   Membership

★ ★ ★ ★ ★ ★ ★ ★ ★   *The American President*
Episode 2: "Happenstance"

episode menu

TYLER ⋈ FILLMORE ⋈ A. JOHNSON ⋈ ARTHUR ⋈ TRUMAN ⋈

Eight vice presidents have been thrust into the high office upon the death of a sitting president. Often underqualified and ill prepared, they became known in their times as "the accidental presidents."

Home ⋈ The Voting Booth ⋈ Resources ⋈ About the Series ⋈ Credits ⋈ thirteen WNET New York PBS

Internet

▲ John Tyler, Harrison's vice president, succeeded Harrison as president. Tyler was the first vice president to be thrust into the presidency because his predecessor had died while in office.

president" or the "ex-vice president." But Tyler would have none of it. His response was to return unopened any mail that was not addressed to the president.[1]

Reorganizing

The days following Harrison's funeral were busy and stressful for John Tyler, both at work and at home. His wife was gravely ill. Letitia had been confined to her bed since suffering a stroke in 1838. Priscilla Tyler, the wife of the Tylers' eldest son, agreed to serve as hostess in place of her mother-in-law. With his home life so difficult, Tyler strove for familiarity in the executive branch. He decided to keep all of Harrison's cabinet.

But his decision to do so did not ensure a stable transition. Immediately, Tyler met resistance. The issue of a national bank was again at the root. Whig leader Henry Clay introduced bills to increase tariffs and recharter the national bank. Although Congress passed the measures, Tyler opposed them and vetoed the bills. This outraged Clay and the whole Whig party, which disowned Tyler as a member. "I will live to be a hundred years," vowed Clay, "and devote them all to the extermination of Tyler and his friends!"[2] As a result, every single member of the cabinet resigned, except for Secretary of State Daniel Webster.

Tyler quickly reorganized his cabinet. Amid strong opposition, he moved to balance the federal budget and reduce public debt. Although he had opposed tariff bills in the past, Tyler signed into law a bill that would charge a new tariff and inject new money into the federal treasury. And with Secretary of State Webster in charge of the negotiations, Tyler's administration successfully ended a boundary dispute between Maine and Canada with the

signing of the Webster-Ashburton Treaty of 1842. This treaty established a northern border for the country as far west as the Rocky Mountains and ensured that westward expansion would continue.

Crossing Borders

But with the opening of the West came trouble along the country's southern border. Texas, which had declared its independence from Mexico in 1836, was still not part of

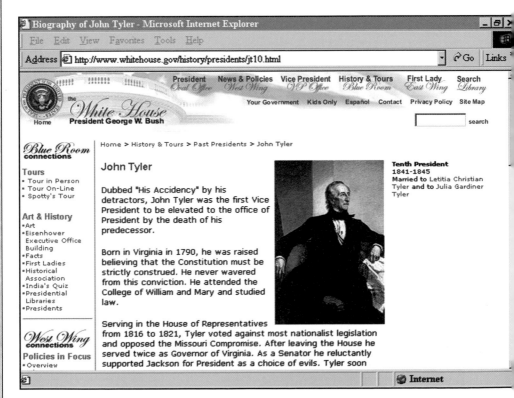

Though he had begun his presidency by being referred to as "His Accidency," John Tyler took his responsibilities as the leader of the country very seriously. His administration was able to balance the budget, reduce public debt, settle a border dispute with Canada, and bring about the end of the Second Seminole War.

the Union. And another war with the Seminole had begun because Jackson supported moving Florida Indians out west if they lived in areas that white people desired. Tyler worked toward a peaceful end to what he called the "vexatious, harassing, and expensive war which so long prevailed with the Indian tribes inhabiting the peninsula of Florida."[3] Tyler was able to bring about the end of the Second Seminole War, in 1842, with the result that most Seminole were forced out of their land forever.

With Tyler's victories as president, however, came a great personal loss. His wife, Letitia, after battling illness for many years, died on September 10, 1842. In a presidency of firsts, Letitia's death marked the first time a first lady had died during the presidency. Her last act was to

▲ This photograph of the White House, taken in the 1840s, shows the Executive Mansion as it looked when John and Letitia Tyler, and then John and Julia Tyler, were its occupants.

take a rose from a bedside vase and hold it in her hand as she passed away.

To deal with his grief, Tyler threw himself into the presidency. His sights were broad. Not only did he want to expand the nation, he also wanted to expand international trade and he focused on China. Although Americans had been sailing into the Chinese port of Canton since 1784, in August 1842 the Treaty of Nanking opened four additional ports to British traders. Tyler had already succeeded in protecting Hawaii (then known as the Sandwich Islands) from British and French control. Now the United States wanted to enjoy more of the fruits of trade with China, which the British had already sampled. In 1844, the Treaty of Wanghia was signed with China, opening Chinese ports to American traders. This also paved the way for the "open door" trade policies that exist to this day.

▶ "The Rose of Long Island"

Within a year of Letitia's death, Tyler met the woman who was to become his second wife. In February 1843, the Gardiners of Long Island, New York—a family of great wealth and stature—were among the guests at a White House dinner. Included in the Gardiner party was daughter Julia, a young woman of beauty, grace, and intelligence. A few years earlier, Julia Gardiner had posed as a model in an advertisement for a New York merchant. The photo caption declared that she was the "Rose of Long Island." In December 1842, another newspaper called her "one of the loveliest women in the United States."[4]

John Tyler certainly thought so when he met her at the White House dinner. He and Julia laughed and played cards like old friends. Two weeks later, he proposed marriage. But she did not accept right away because she was concerned about the age difference. At fifty-two, Tyler was more than thirty years older than Julia. But Tyler continued to send her love letters.

Unfortunately, it was tragedy that drew the couple closer. In February 1844, Tyler, members of his cabinet, Julia and her father, David Gardiner, and others boarded the *Princeton*, a new steam warship, to inspects its propellers and a gun known as the Peacemaker. As the ship sailed down the Potomac River, people proposed toasts and sang songs. But without warning, the Peacemaker

Biography of Julia Tyler - Microsoft Internet Explorer

File Edit View Favorites Tools Help

Address http://www.whitehouse.gov/history/firstladies/jt10.html   Go   Links

President   News & Policies   Vice President   History & Tours   First Lady   Search
Oval Office   West Wing   VP Office   Blue Room   East Wing   Library

the White House   Your Government Kids Only Español Contact Privacy Policy Site Map
Home   President George W. Bush   search

Blue Room
connections   Home > History & Tours > Past First Ladies > Julia Gardiner Tyler

Tours   Julia Gardiner Tyler   Lived: 1820-1889
• Tour in Person
• Tour On-Line   "I grieve my love a belle should be," sighed   Mrs. John Tyler.
• Spotty's Tour   one of Julia Gardiner's innumerable admirers
                         in 1840; at the age of 20 she was already
Art & History   famous as the "Rose of Long Island."
• Art
• Eisenhower   Daughter of Juliana McLachlan and David
  Executive Office   Gardiner, descendant of prominent and
  Building   wealthy New York families, Julia was trained
• Facts   from earliest childhood for a life in society;
• First Ladies   she made her debut at 15. A European tour
• Historical   with her family gave her new glimpses of
  Association   social splendors. Late in 1842 the Gardiners
• India's Quiz   went to Washington for the winter social season, and Julia became
• Presidential   the undisputed darling of the capital. Her beauty and her practiced
  Libraries   charm attracted the most eminent men in the city, among them
• Presidents   President Tyler, a widower since September.

West Wing   Tragedy brought his courtship poignant success the next winter.
connections

Policies in Focus
• Overview

                                                                    Internet

A newspaper account described Julia Gardiner, John Tyler's second wife, as "one of the loveliest women in the United States." It was Julia Gardiner Tyler who began the tradition of "Hail to the Chief" being played at presidential functions.

exploded. Eight people on board were killed, including two cabinet secretaries and David Gardiner, the man who would have become Tyler's father-in-law. Julia, who had been below deck at the time of the explosion, fainted when she heard the news of her father's death, and Tyler had to carry her to the rescue boat.

Though Julia was in mourning, she also realized that marrying Tyler would lift her spirits. "After I lost my father," she recalled, "I felt differently toward the President. He seemed . . . to be more agreeable in every way than any younger man ever was or could be."[5] In June 1844, John Tyler and Julia Gardiner were married. He was the first president to marry while in office. Although some snickered about the age difference, many admirers thought Tyler had made a good choice. Julia was beautiful, wealthy, and a gracious first lady. Tyler and his new wife immediately redecorated the White House, which was then in shabby condition, so that Julia could host grand parties in an elegant setting. Julia also began the tradition of having "Hail to the Chief" played whenever the president appeared at national functions.

▶ The Annexation of Texas

Julia also supported Tyler's political positions, such as the lingering question about the annexation of Texas. Texas had requested the federal government to consider annexation back in 1837. By 1844, Tyler was ready to move the issue to the forefront of his reelection campaign. He viewed annexation as critical. But Mexican President Antonio Lopez de Santa Anna warned that the annexation of Texas would mean war, because Mexico did not recognize Texas's independence. Tyler wanted to find a way to annex Texas and appease Santa Anna at the same time.

▲ On March 4, 1845, John Tyler's presidency came to a close, but not before he had succeeded in signing a joint congressional resolution to annex Texas. Texas would not officially become a state until December 1845, nine months after Tyler's term had ended.

Tyler was also concerned that because Texas would enter the Union a slave state, Congress would not approve its annexation.

Tyler attempted to run for president again on the Democratic ticket, but he could not gather enough support. The party nominated James K. Polk instead, and the Democrats adopted the Texas issue for themselves. The result was Polk's victory in the election of 1844. While preparing for the transition to a new administration, Tyler took Polk's election as a signal that the American people wanted Texas to be part of the United States. He suggested a congressional resolution to annex Texas, which Congress passed. Just three days before he left the White House, Tyler signed the measure into law. He then gave the historic pen to Julia, who wore it around her neck. Just one day before he left office, Tyler signed a bill admitting Florida to the Union. Texas would not become a state until December 19, 1845—after Tyler's term but in large part due to Tyler's efforts.

On March 4, 1845, Tyler rode with the Polks in the inaugural carriage. After four busy years marked by both triumph and sadness, Tyler's presidency was over. "In 1840 I was called from my farm to undertake the administration of public affairs, and I foresaw that I was called to a bed of thorns," Tyler remarked. "I now leave that bed which has afforded me little rest, and eagerly seek repose in the quiet enjoyments of rural life."[6]

Chapter 5 ▶

Tyler's Legacy, 1845–1862

Although Julia wanted to stay in Washington long enough to attend the Polk inaugural ball, Tyler was eager to go home. He did not want to leave the White House and spend the night in a hotel, so he and Julia

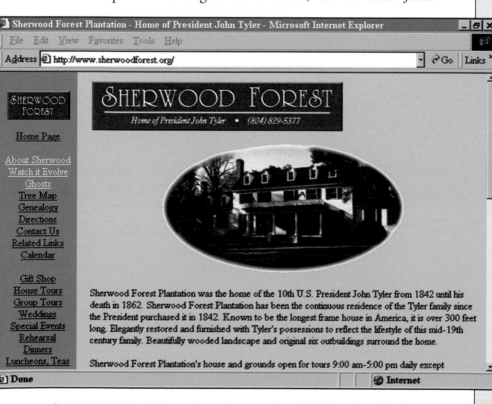

SHERWOOD FOREST

Home of President John Tyler • (804) 829-5377

Sherwood Forest Plantation was the home of the 10th U.S. President John Tyler from 1842 until his death in 1862. Sherwood Forest Plantation has been the continuous residence of the Tyler family since the President purchased it in 1842. Known to be the longest frame house in America, it is over 300 feet long. Elegantly restored and furnished with Tyler's possessions to reflect the lifestyle of this mid-19th century family. Beautifully wooded landscape and original six outbuildings surround the home.

Sherwood Forest Plantation's house and grounds open for tours 9:00 am-5:00 pm daily except

▲ In 1842, John Tyler purchased a sprawling plantation along the James River, only three miles from Greenway, his childhood home. He named his new estate "Sherwood Forest," and he added a 68-foot ballroom to it so that he and Julia and their friends could enjoy the Virginia reel, a popular dance of the day.

immediately left the capital to retire to Sherwood Forest, Tyler's Virginia plantation.

Located only three miles from his beloved Greenway, Sherwood Forest was a sprawling plantation along the James River that Tyler had purchased in 1842. The home was known formally as "The Grove," but Tyler renamed it "Sherwood Forest" after Robin Hood's woodland retreat. Tyler fancied himself something of an outlaw, like the mythical Robin Hood, following his own belief system even if it made him enemies.

In 1845, Tyler added a 68-foot ballroom to their home so that Julia and their friends could perform a popular dance of the time, the Virginia reel. At more than 300 feet long, Sherwood Forest remains the longest frame house in America. Overlooking terraced gardens and lawns, it was a peaceful place to raise a growing family. Between 1846 and 1860, Julia bore seven children. In his lifetime, Tyler fathered fifteen children, more than any other president.

Tyler enjoyed a quiet home life. He could often be seen on horseback, wearing a wide-brimmed hat, as he supervised the farming of fruits, potatoes, grain, and corn on his estate. Although he kept slaves, Tyler referred to them as "servants," gave them adequate clothing and shelter, and kept families together. As his farming operations grew, Tyler started hiring freedmen to work alongside his slaves. This arrangement continued until the outbreak of the Civil War.

Though retired, Tyler still followed national events. In 1846, a year after he left the White House, the annexation of Texas led to the Mexican War. The conflict arose from a dispute over the border between the United States and Mexico. Although Tyler thought war could have been avoided, he supported a strong show of force against

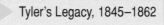

Genealogy of John Tyler at Sherwood Forest Plantation - Home of President John Tyler - Microsoft Internet Explorer

File Edit View Favorites Tools Help

Links »

Address http://www.sherwoodforest.org/Genealogy.html

Home Page

About
Sherwood
Watch it Evolve
Ghosts
Tree Map
Genealogy
Directions
Contact Us
Related Links
Calendar

Gift Shop
House Tours
Group Tours
Weddings
Special Events
Rehearsal
Dinners

John Tyler   *Julia Gardiner Tyler*

Genealogy of John Tyler and his Descendants

John Tyler was the most prolific of all American President: he had 15 children and two wives. In 1813, Tyler married Letitia Christian, the daughter of a Virginia planter. They had eight children. She was an invalid when Tyler became president and made only one public appearance, at her daughter Elizabeth's marriage in 1842. Letitia Christian Tyler, the President's first wife, died in the White House in September, 1842. A few months later, Tyler began courting 23-year-old Julia Gardiner, a beautiful and wealthy New

Internet

In his lifetime, John Tyler fathered fifteen children—eight with his first wife, Letitia, and seven with his second wife, Julia.

Mexico. Julia was interested as well, writing to her brothers about the "courage and valor" of the soldiers. In 1848, the Treaty of Guadalupe Hidalgo ended the war, and the border between the United States and Mexico was fixed at the Rio Grande.

Tyler's support for states' rights never wavered throughout his life. He strongly opposed the idea that Congress could restrict slavery in new territories. And he was outraged when an abolitionist named John Brown raided a federal arsenal in Harpers Ferry, Virginia, and called for the armed revolt of all Virginia slaves. When

Abraham Lincoln was elected president in 1860, tensions between North and South were at the breaking point. Several states, led by South Carolina, began to secede from the Union. In February 1861, Tyler was asked to serve as chairman of a peace convention created to avoid a civil war. Although he made several speeches calling for peace, and traveled to Washington to attend the convention's meeting, it was clear to Tyler that the states of the deep South intended to leave the Union.

Tyler returned to Sherwood Forest, his feelings in turmoil. Although he supported slavery and states' rights, he had served the United States and the U.S. Constitution his entire life. In early 1861, Tyler made the difficult decision to support Virginia's decision to secede from the Union. "These are dark times, dearest, and I think only of you and our little ones," he wrote Julia. "I shall vote secession."[1]

▶ A Confederate End

In 1861, Tyler was elected first to the temporary Confederate Congress and then to the Confederate House of Representatives. He became the only U.S. president to hold office in the Confederacy. When he traveled to Richmond to attend the first session of the Confederate Congress, Julia had a disturbing dream. In it, Tyler looked pale and ill. Julia was so disturbed by the dream that she rushed to her husband's side. At first, he chuckled at her concerns. Later, however, he felt sick, cold, and dizzy and told Julia that her dream had come true. On January 18, 1862, with doctors and friends all around him, Tyler died, right before he was to begin the last job of his political life. Among his final words to his wife were "Love piled on love will not convey an idea of my affection for you."[2]

On January 20, several thousand mourners filed past his casket in the black-draped Confederate Congress building. He was later buried in Hollywood Cemetery in Richmond. But because Tyler had died as a Confederate, many in Washington and in the North considered him a traitor. For many decades afterward, John Tyler would be regarded as one of the nation's least effective presidents. More than fifty years passed before the U.S. Congress recognized his death, with a monument in Hollywood Cemetery.

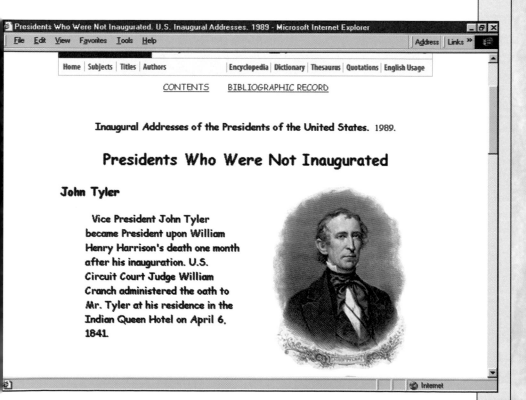

Presidents Who Were Not Inaugurated. U.S. Inaugural Addresses. 1989 - Microsoft Internet Explorer

File Edit View Favorites Tools Help

Address | Links »

Home | Subjects | Titles | Authors | Encyclopedia | Dictionary | Thesaurus | Quotations | English Usage

CONTENTS   BIBLIOGRAPHIC RECORD

Inaugural Addresses of the Presidents of the United States. 1989.

Presidents Who Were Not Inaugurated

John Tyler

Vice President John Tyler became President upon William Henry Harrison's death one month after his inauguration. U.S. Circuit Court Judge William Cranch administered the oath to Mr. Tyler at his residence in the Indian Queen Hotel on April 6, 1841.

John Tyler was one of five U.S. presidents who, because of the circumstances of their succession to the presidency, were not inaugurated. The other four were Millard Fillmore, Andrew Johnson, Chester A. Arthur, and Gerald R. Ford.

But views toward our tenth president have softened somewhat. His efforts to strengthen and expand the nation resulted in Texas and Florida becoming states and in greater international trade. And some historians point to Tyler's succession to the presidency after Harrison's death as perhaps his most important legacy. It firmly established the right of the vice president to succeed the president in such circumstances.

Chapter Notes

Chapter 1. The Accidental President

1. Paul F. Boller, Jr., *Presidential Anecdotes* (New York: Oxford University Press, 1981), pp. 95–98.

Chapter 2. Tyler's Early Life, 1790–1809

1. Robert Seager II, *And Tyler Too: A Biography of John and Julia Gardiner Tyler* (New York: McGraw-Hill Book Company, 1963), p. 49.

2. Oliver Perry Chitwood, *John Tyler: Champion of the Old South* (Newtown, Conn.: American Political Biography Press, 1996. Reprint of a 1939 edition published by the American Historical Association), p. 15.

Chapter 3. Journey to the White House, 1811–1841

1. Robert Seager II, *And Tyler Too: A Biography of John and Julia Gardiner Tyler* (New York: McGraw-Hill Book Company, 1963), p. 56.

2. Ibid., p. 59.

3. Ibid., p. 60.

4. Ibid., p. 56.

5. Ibid., p. 82.

6. Ibid., p. 140.

Chapter 4. A Bed of Thorns: The Presidency, 1841–1845

1. Robert Seager II, *And Tyler Too: A Biography of John and Julia Gardiner Tyler* (New York: McGraw-Hill Book Company, 1963), p. 149.

2. Dee Lillegard, *John Tyler: Tenth President of the United States* (Chicago: Children's Press, 1987), p. 56.

3. Norma Lois Peterson, *The Presidencies of William Henry Harrison & John Tyler* (Lawrence, Kans.: University Press of Kansas, 1989), p. 271.

4. Seager II, p. 184.

5. Paul F. Boller, Jr., *Presidential Wives: An Anecdotal History* (New York: Oxford University Press, 1989), p. 82.

6. Seager II, p. 291.

Chapter 5. Tyler's Legacy, 1845–1862

1. Robert Seager II, *And Tyler Too: A Biography of John and Julia Gardiner Tyler* (New York: McGraw-Hill Book Company, 1963), p. 447.

2. Ibid., p. 471.

Further Reading

Bassett, Margaret. *Profiles and Portraits of American Presidents.* New York: David McKay Company, 1976.

Boller, Paul F., Jr. *Presidential Anecdotes.* New York: Oxford University Press, 1981.

_____. *Presidential Wives: An Anecdotal History.* New York: Oxford University Press, 1989.

Chitwood, Oliver Perry. *John Tyler: Champion of the Old South.* Newtown, Conn.: American Political Biography Press, 1996. Reprint of a 1939 edition published by the American Historical Association.

Falkof, Lucille, and Richard G. Young., eds. *John Tyler: Tenth President of the United States.* Ada, Okla.: Garrett Educational Corporation, 1990.

Lillegard, Dee. *John Tyler: Tenth President of the United States.* Chicago: Children's Press, 1987.

Peterson, Norma Lois. *The Presidencies of William Henry Harrison & John Tyler.* Lawrence, Kans.: University Press of Kansas, 1989.

Seager II, Robert. *And Tyler Too: A Biography of John and Julia Gardiner Tyler.* New York: McGraw-Hill Book Company, 1963.

Walker, Jane C. *John Tyler: President of Many Firsts.* Granville, Ohio.: The McDonald & Woodward Publishing Company, 2001.

Weber, Michael. *Jackson, Van Buren, Harrison, Tyler & Polk.* Vero Beach, Fla.: Rourke Corporation, Division of Rourke Publishing Group, 1996.

Welsbacher, Anne. *John Tyler.* Minneapolis, Minn.: ABDO Publishing Company, 2000.

Franklin Pierce College Library

00137328

DATE DUE

GAYLORD

PRINTED IN U.S.A.